NEGOTIATING A PERMEABLE CURRICULUM: ON LITERACY, DIVERSITY, AND THE INTERPLAY OF CHILDREN'S AND TEACHERS' WORLDS

NEGOTIATING A PERMEABLE CURRICULUM: ON LITERACY, DIVERSITY, AND THE INTERPLAY OF CHILDREN'S AND TEACHERS' WORLDS

ANNE HAAS DYSON

GARN PRESS WOMEN SCHOLARS SERIES

BOBBIE KABUTO, SENIOR EDITOR

GARN PRESS
NEW YORK, NY

Published by Garn Press, LLC
New York, NY
www.garnpress.com

The chapter of this book titled *Negotiating a Permeable Curriculum: On Literacy, Diversity, and the Interplay of Children's and Teachers' Worlds* by Anne Haas Dyson was previously published as Concept Paper No. 9 by the National Council of Teachers of English (NCTE), copyright © 1993, and is reprinted here by permission.

Book and cover design by Benjamin J. Taylor/Garn Press
Cover drawing by Samuel K., used with permission.

Library of Congress Control Number: 2016943571

Publisher's Cataloging-in-Publication Data

Names: Dyson, Anne Haas | Kabuto, Bobbie.
Title: Negotiating a permeable curriculum : on literacy, diversity,
    and the interplay of children's and teachers' worlds / Anne Haas
    Dyson and Bobbie Kabuto (editor).
Description: New York : Garn Press, 2016
Identifiers: LCCN 2016943571 | ISBN 978-1-942146-43-8 (pbk.)
Subjects: LCSH: Education--Curricula. | Education, Elementary. |
    Teaching--Principles and practice. | Language arts (Elementary).
    | Social Sciences--Study and teaching (Elementary). | BISAC:
    EDUCATION / Curricula. | EDUCATION / Elementary. |
    EDUCATION / Teaching Methods & Materials / General. |
    EDUCATION / Teaching Methods & Materials / Language Arts.
    | EDUCATION / Teaching Methods & Materials / Social Science.
Classification: LCC LB1576 D974 2016 (print) | DDC
    372.196/9940092--dc23.

For my mother,

Athleen Weiske Haas

Who taught me that everyone has a story

*Schools declare themselves as surely as people
do. And children learn to read the implicit
meanings... "What does this place say to me?"
they ask.... In finding the answer they also
discover what it is possible for them to say.*

Connie and Harold Rosen, 1973
The language of primary school children
**London: Schools Council Publications/
Penguin Education**

Contents

Introduction

Bobbie Kabuto

Curriculum is the heart and soul of educational systems, and it is in jeopardy of a coup d'état by corporate and political forces. It has not always been this way. As a teacher in the mid 1990s, I knew a time when money was invested in the professional development of teachers rather in high-stakes testing. States possessed state curricular standards, and teachers were directly invested in collaborative planning. Curriculum development and mapping were the major foci of the regular professional development workshops in which I participated. Our first priority was not teaching to national standards or for our students to pass state tests, it was about developmentally and culturally appropriate teaching. It was about knowing our students and looking at them as social beings who bring varied levels of understanding and background knowledge to the curriculum. Teaching was about creating a dynamic, dialogic curricular model in which students were engaged and worked at their individual levels of understanding.

It is not all that surprising that the research in the 1990s in language and literacy, focused on a humanistic pedagogy, made an influential impact on me as a teacher and, later, an as educational researcher and scholar. It is, therefore, with great pleasure that I introduce Anne Haas Dyson, who will be the focus of this volume as part of the Garn Press Women Scholars Series. Dyson's seminal work and prolific writings on childhood writers began in the early 1980s and continues to this day.

Originally published in 1993 in the National Council of Teachers of English (NCTE) Concept Paper Series, *Negotiating a Permeable Curriculum: On Literacy, Diversity, and the Interplay of Children's and Teachers' Worlds* revisits Dyson's powerful concept of a permeable curriculum. According to Dyson, a permeable curriculum is more than a set of content standards and objectives, it is a socially constructed learning space created by teachers and children. Dyson (1993a) writes of a permeable curriculum, "Such a shared world is essential for the growth of both oral and written language, and it is essential as well if teachers and children are to feel connected to, not alienated from, each other" (p. 1).

Thus, through the creation of a shared space, the curriculum is no longer identified as a set of skills and ideas that needs to be transmitted from the more knowledgeable teacher to the inexperienced student. Instead, children are positioned as social negotiators as "they explore and exploit the power of symbolic tools as social mediators" (Dyson, 1993a, p. 4). Curriculum is negotiated between teacher and student. As Dyson (1993a) argues, "the worlds of the teachers and children come together in instructionally powerful ways" (p. 3).

Dyson's words stand in stark contrast to the current moves in education with the implementation of the Common Core State Standards (CCSS). Much has changed since I was a teacher in 1995. In 2010, the CCSS were released as a set of standards devised to create national benchmarks of student knowledge and skills in literacy and math. While not specifically mentioning curriculum, the CCSS explicitly outlines what should be taught from kindergarten to grade 12, and they have in fact had a major impact in establishing a national curriculum and assessment system led by private, corporate companies.

Researchers and grassroots movements from parents, students, and community leaders have tirelessly challenged the motivation, necessity, and reliability of the CCSS in creating college- and career-ready students, as well as questioning the privatization of education. Opponents of the CCSS call for more local autonomy in establishing curricular standards in their schools and school districts. These recent political, corporate, and grassroots changes in education make the revisiting of Dyson's permeable curriculum timely and necessary.

In what follows, I will introduce the reader to three tenets that build a foundation for *Negotiating a Permeable Curriculum*. I will do so through the voice and world of a child writer, my son Ricky, who I observed learning to write from the time he picked up a plastic eggroll from his kitchen set at 2 years old thinking that he could use it to mark on a piece of paper, to the present time when writing is now about finding evidence in the passage to support the main idea of his paragraph. So here I return to Ricky's second-grade year to examine the social worlds of the child composer and the official world of school, as well as the impact that the curriculum had in positioning Ricky as a struggling learner.

Composing Through Form and Function

Writing is a symbolic tool that children learn to employ in order to navigate through their social worlds before they learn to fully control the tool itself. The early research on beginning writing – by researchers such as Denny Taylor (1983) in *Family Literacy*, Jerome Harste, V. Woodward, and Carolyn Burke (1984) in *Language Stories & Literacy Lessons*, and Marcia Baghban (1984) in *Our Daughter Learns to Read and Write* – focused on close observations of young children learning to write. This body of early research contributed to our understandings of two aspects of writing – learning conventional written language forms and employing written language for complex social functions.

"Conventional written language forms" refers to the written forms that compose a writing system. For instance, the English language uses the Roman alphabet as its written language form, while Chinese uses Chinese *kanji* (Chinese characters) as its written form. While learning how to form letters that make up the Roman alphabet is one entry point in learning to write, children also learn a variety of social conventions that guide how they use the written forms. Children learn to use a capital letter to begin a sentence and to capitalize the first letter of a proper noun, like in a name. The term, "social convention," connects to the idea that written language forms are given meaning by social and cultural guidelines, or conventions. Therefore, when children begin to make marks on a piece of paper or write a letter on a page, they are learning how to participate in a larger social and cultural structure that gives meaning to the marks that they make.

This notion is particularly important when we think about social and cultural diversity, and how more experienced writers, like teachers, interpret the writing of novice writers. For instance, both the English and Spanish languages use the Roman alphabet for their written language form. While this may be the case, each language is comprised of a different system of sounds. Speakers of English apply the English sound system, or phonology, to the Roman alphabet, while Spanish speakers apply the Spanish sound system. A bilingual English- and Spanish-speaking child, who has a range of linguistic resources, applies a range of sound systems based on the English and Spanish phonology to the Roman alphabet when spelling and writing.

To provide an example, a teacher who was in my graduate class was quite perplexed as to why a bilingual child wrote the following sentence, "My brother is 10 years old," as "Mai prasr ev 10 ya ot." The teacher felt that the bilingual child was "confused" because his Spanish interfered with his English writing, and wondered if there was a possible learning disability. This, in fact, was not the case, and there are linguistic reasons to explain the child's writing behaviors. This bilingual speaker applied his knowledge of the Spanish and English phonology to the Roman alphabet when spelling words.

I refer to these types of linguistic behaviors as part of translanguaging, which denotes the dynamic nature of language and counters the additive approach to bilingualism and biliteracy (Garcia & Wei, 2014). Translanguaging does not position Languages (I use the capital *L* to denote language in its formalized sense) as separate autonomous systems (i.e. a Spanish Language or an English Language), as language can transcend traditional bounded forms. The writing of this bilingual student was aimed at communicating a message and, in order to communicate that message, he needed to break down traditional language boundaries.

While this may be the case, the teacher interpreted the child's bilingual writing behavior through a deficit-oriented perspective. Her concern was about the surface features of the writing, in particular his spelling, and spelling is not synonymous with writing. Without realizing it, this teacher was in the process of socially constructing an identity for this bilingual writer that positioned him as "at-risk" and "confused." Dyson (1993a) describes the challenges that teachers like this one face:

> "Indeed, research in schools serving children from diverse sociocultural backgrounds suggests that teachers and children often do feel disconnected, a feeling exacerbated by differences in race and class" (p. 1).

Teachers who enact a permeable curriculum reject that idea that students like this bilingual student need to fit into neat categories, and follow a predicted line of developmental learning when learning the range of surface features of writing, which includes spelling, grammar, and handwriting.

Becoming a writer, however, is not only about learning written language forms and social conventions that guide the use of those forms. It is also about social enactments, or functions. The research and writings of Dyson have made a major impact in understanding how writing is about "taking action, of entering into a social dialogue" into which the youngest of writers can engage (Dyson, 1993a, p.6).

Dyson (1993a) argues, "As teachers, then, we must attend to much more than children's invented words on a page, for writing is not just a specialized way of marking (although it's that, too)" (p. 6). While children do need to learn the conventional forms of written language and social conventions, learning to write is about learning about the world – the people, places, and things that make up the world – and being someone who engages in it.

To illustrate this point, I go back in time to when Ricky was 7 years old and in the second grade. Ricky, who was an avid *Mario Cart* player, liked to challenge his uncle in an occasional, friendly game. During a visit to his aunt and uncle's house, the friendly game became a little competitive, and when $10 was on the line for winning, Ricky decided to draw up a contract (see Figure 1).

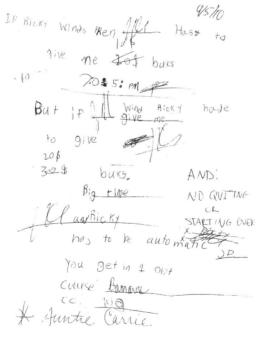

Figure 1. Ricky's *Mario Cart* Contract.

Ricky wrote, "If Ricky wins, then ___ (his uncle initialed) has to give me $20 (which Ricky crossed out because his uncle would not agree and wrote $10) $10 bucks. But if ___ (his uncle initialed) wins Ricky has (to) give me $30 (which Ricky crossed out because I would not agree and wrote $20) $20 bucks." There are several stipulations listed in the contract, which Ricky's aunt added. They are (1) no quitting, (2) no starting over, (3) the car has to be an automatic one, and (4) the course and distance. Both Ricky and his uncle initialed and signed to recognize the stipulations.

This example illustrates how writing was the result of "joint constructions" by the participating members of Ricky's social circle as it served the goal of creating a "social cohesion" (Dyson, 1993b, p. 59). There is evidence in this piece of writing of Ricky learning how to control the social conventions of written language, such as spelling, but Ricky was not constrained by writing "correctly" and, thus, was able to use written language to communicate a socially meaningful message.

In *Social Worlds of Children Learning to Write*, Dyson (1993b) writes, "Writing, like all language use, is always a situated response, an addressing of another in a particular time and place, a motivated making of words for some end" (p. 217). Through the creation of the contract, Ricky could exercise control and agency within the space – his contract was a situated response to meet some end. The relationships through and around the written language were authentic, not generic, and they were permeable, as the individuals involved had invested interests in the outcome of the writing.

Dyson (1993a) cautions about creating a generic nature to pedagogy when she writes, "Moreover, making use of children's social intelligence entails rethinking the generic nature of writing pedagogy for young children" (p. 29). She continues, "Considering children as social actors thus suggests that 'audience,' 'editor,' and 'response' are situated, not generic, terms that can be explicitly discussed and planned for children" (p. 29). Within Ricky's *Mario Cart* contract all participants acted as audience, editor, and responder, and they actively constructed an authentic space that gave meaning to the contract and their relationships with each other.

The Official and Unofficial Worlds of Child Writers

Ricky constructed the *Mario Cart* contract within the natural context of the family, or in a space within the "home world" (Dyson, 1993b, p. 54). Researchers (e.g. Maderazo, 2014) have documented how writing within the home can differ from the types of writing activities produced in school, potentially positioning children as having learning difficulties. While the home environment supports everyday contextualized writing, writing in school is often decontextualized – pulled apart so that children are forced to work with written language forms and social conventions in a meaningless manner.

Describing writing pedagogy, Dyson (1993a) argues that "pedagogical writing about child literacy often assumes that the developmental goal is 'decontextualized' written language, that is, language in which ideas are made explicit in tightly constructed prose, rather than implicitly understood by familiar interlocutors" (p. 29). And yet children like Ricky find ways to work outside of the official worlds of school when writing.

Another example of Ricky's writing that occurred in the home during his second grade year is his authored book *The Apple, Book 1* (see Figure 2, Ricky wrote four books in his *The Apple* series). On separate sheets of paper, Ricky wrote the text and drew the pictures page by page. The book reads as follows:

Page 1: The apple. It was small. I eat apples.

Page 2: But here comes the wind. The apple could fall off.

Page 3: The wind was so fast it made the apple fell

Page 4: Poor apple. It's all alone.

Page 5: But someone is coming. He could eat the apple.

Page 6: It is a he. He was getting the apple.

Page 7: He eat the apple. It was so delicious. Now his apple was his favorite.

Page 8: He eat the fall apple. The End.

Figure 2: Ricky's *The Apple Book*

Paying close attention to how illustrations also tell a story, Ricky drew his illustrations to match his written text. For instance, when Ricky wrote about the wind, he drew short horizontal, blue lines across the page, and when the wind blew the apple, he drew the apple in the air falling from the tree. After Ricky finished with the text and illustrations, he cut the pages so he could make a small book. What Ricky enjoyed the most, however, was reading the book to me. His book was not just a book because he tried to make it look like one. It was a book because he could share it with me and other people. Ricky went on to write three more books in the series, and other books like his nonfiction book, *What is a Plane?*, and his fictional stories, *The Gingerbread Guy* and *The Little Candy Cane*.

He wrote the last two books in his third-grade year, starting each book at home to bring to school, crossing the boundaries of home and school. Once Ricky brought the book to school, it entered into what Dyson (1993b) terms as the unofficial world of the classroom. Ricky's classroom friends became characters in the book, took on different characteristics, and engaged in dramatic events. For instance, Ricky's friend Tommy became Tom Gingerbread who was the "sneakiest guy at Gingerbread World."

In collaborating in the creation of the books, Ricky's friends jointly created an imaginative world where each person could take on alternative identities, or as Dyson would describe, the joint construction of *The Gingerbread Guy* developed a social cohesion within Ricky's peer world. Ricky and his friends worked on his book between official classroom routines, especially over the indoor recess time when they spent time in the classroom because of the cold New York winters. As Dyson (1993b) explains, while teachers organize the official classroom routines, children organize the unofficial worlds, which are "formed in response to adult-governed worlds, but they were collaboratively enacted within the life space of the children" (p. 52).

Similar to what Dyson (1993b) found, the unofficial spaces that Ricky created with his books were "socially dramatic places, where children worked hard to proclaim their own uniqueness in ways that would gain the respect of others" (p. 66). For Ricky, these spaces did not always fit into the official world of school nor were they always accepted by his teachers. Often, Ricky's books did not count towards assessing and evaluating Ricky's reading and writing performances, because the books were not considered part of the school's official space and were either forgotten or simply ignored.

Rigidity and Permeability

Ricky's second-grade year was a particularly challenging one for Ricky. Examining the social worlds and the unofficial spaces within which Ricky participated highlights the ways in which he used writing as a tool to navigate his social worlds as well as the people and actions embedded within them. Ricky's difficulty was not necessarily with his underlying ability to read and write, it was the ways in which the rigidity of the curriculum, and how his teachers interpreted the curriculum, positioned him as a struggling learner.

The official world of school was about the forms and conventions of written language. Children who mastered those two pieces of written language were deemed as better readers and writers than children who did not. In the second grade, Ricky's primary work around reading and writing was through the school reading specialist rather than through his classroom teacher. While I never saw or received an in-depth report from Ricky's classroom teacher for reading and writing, I received one from the reading specialist at my request. The reading specialist provided me with the following conclusions from Ricky's January, 2010 assessment:

- Ricky reflected limited understanding of the text he read. He mentioned a few facts or ideas but did not express the important information or ideas.

- Ricky's decoding is on grade level.

- Ricky's comprehension is weak using the GRADE (assessment) and Running Record.

- Ricky's word knowledge score was weak using the Gates-MacGinitie assessment.

Based on this assessment report, Ricky's reading specialist recommended him to the Intervention Services Team (IST) who would determine if Ricky needed further school interventions. After their initial meeting, of which I was not notified, the school speech and language specialist contacted me for permission for speech and language testing. At this point, my intervention was the turning point in Ricky's second grade year, and I called for an immediate halt of further testing or even talk of further testing.

When I received Ricky's assessment results in April of his second-grade year, however, there was the same discourse by the reading specialist as she noted the following:

- Ricky reflected a limited understanding of the text he read. He mentioned a few facts or ideas but did not express the important information or ideas.

- Ricky's comprehension remains a concern.

- Ricky reflected no understanding of the text when he was asked to write about the story.

For the last point, Ricky was asked to read a story and write from the point of view of one of the characters. Ricky was asked to write three behaviors that the character found annoying and to compare those behaviors to another character. Ricky wrote verbatim:

They both like swimming.

They are both messy.

They like to away's like to go outside.

I do not deny that Ricky's responses to the written questions did not fully address the questions and, most likely, did not demonstrate his understanding of the story. Ricky's performances on these tasks, however, are in stark contrast to his performances when creating the *Mario Cart Contract* and *The Apple, Book 1,* and later *The Gingerbread Guy* in his third-grade year. The rigidity of the curriculum in Ricky's classroom during his second-grade year was more reflective of the work of Taylor (1991), who documented how the official world of school constructed the disability of a student.

The perspective of the official world also contrasts with that of Dyson's work, which readers will encounter in this volume. Dyson (1993a) shows us both hope and the possibilities of a permeable curriculum where "teachers with such curiosity talk with (not simply about) parents and community members, seeking insight into children's lives beyond the school walls and into the language use that pervades those lives" (p. 32).

Ricky's teachers played crucial roles in reproducing and perpetuating a perceived learning difficulty by a rigid interpretation of what should be taught, what students should learn, and how they should perform in school. Ricky's teachers did not look "beyond the school walls" to see the complex social and intellectual work that he could do in his growth as a writer and a learner.

The tasks built into the official spaces of school favored the disembodied uses of language. They were generic tasks, particularly the writing tasks, which did not possess a motivated construction of meaning to meet some socially important and oriented goal. What Ricky learned to do well in his home world did not translate to the school world because the world of school presented a different type of writing.

Exploring Ricky's experiences as a learner through the concepts put forth in *Negotiating a Permeable Curriculum* raises the critical question: "When does a learning difficulty become a problem with the curriculum rather than a problem with the child?" In other words, how does a curriculum socially construct the identities and abilities of children like Ricky? I am left wondering what would have happened if the permeability of the curriculum had created a space where Ricky's unofficial world could have entered into the official world of the school? How could the worlds of Ricky's teachers and Ricky come together in "instructionally powerful ways" so that a new space could be created – a transgenerational space where learning transcended the borders of time and space and of teacher-student generations?

Final Thoughts

Applying *Negotiating a Permeable Curriculum* to Ricky's experiences in school 22 years after its original publication date shows that *Negotiating a Permeable Curriculum* is a timeless piece that offers readers a renewed look into what a critical, dialogic pedagogy can look like if enacted in classrooms. The concept of the permeable curriculum has much to offer in thinking about schooling and pedagogy. For me, it provided a lens to think about how curriculum can be a space which can be constructed by teachers and students, and how a non-permeable curriculum can be used to position students and construct sometimes false labels through its rigidity.

Others build on the concept in different ways. Salazar (2013) uses the concept of a permeable curriculum to describe a "humanizing pedagogy" that allows for the "inclusion of students' linguistic, cultural, and social resources" (p. 139). Salazar further explains:

> Educators orienting toward a humanizing pedagogy foster permeability when they accept code switching in student discourse, support heritage-language use as a means of fostering student comprehension, facilitate student input into the curriculum, provide opportunities for students to make personal connections to content, and include topics that reflect the diversity of students' lives. (p. 139)

Other researchers expand on the relationships between a permeable curriculum and linguistic, social, and cultural diversity. Rex (2006) discusses issues of race in classroom interactions, using the concept to better understand how "social identity is enacted and received in the social world and for observing what the intersection of culture, structure, and human agency produces" (p. 315).

Kuby, Rucker, and Kirchhofer (2015) bring forth a discussion of writing within an official curricular space. Similar to Dyson's work, these researchers question students' intentions when participating in Writer's Workshop in a second-grade classroom. They argue:

Dominant discourses in schools, published writing curricula materials and educational standards privilege alphabetic writing. We noticed that children did not always have an end goal in mind when constructing during Writing Workshop. On many occasions, writing was an exploration of bodies, modes and materials in social interactions (p. 3).

Focusing on the role of the teacher, the authors contend that teachers are critical in how children "intra-act" with materials and space when writing in the classroom.

In the conclusion of *Negotiating a Permeable Curriculum*, Dyson talks about pushing back the "curricular curtain" to wonder about the complex social and intellectual work in which children engage when they *become* writers. The emphasis on *becoming* focuses on how learning to write is always a dynamic state, as children learn about themselves while they learn about written language.

When I moved the curricular curtain aside in Ricky's second-grade year, I observed how he saw writing as a tool of the imagination and a way to enact his freedom and control in the complex cartographies that defined his social worlds. As readers enter into *Negotiating a Permeable Curriculum*, I encourage them to push back the curricular curtain that has begun to cloud our senses on what teachers should teach and what students should learn. This is the first step in generating a permeable curriculum where the social and intellectual energy of our students can penetrate into the official classroom worlds.

References

Baghban, M. (1984). *Our daughter learns to read and write: A case study from birth to three*. Newark, DE: International Reading Association.

Dyson, A. H. (1993b). *Social worlds of children learning to write in an urban primary school*. New York, NY: Teachers College Press.

Dyson, A. H. (1993a). Negotiating a permeable curriculum: On literacy, diversity, and the interplay between teachers and children's worlds. Concept Paper. Urbana, IL: NCTE, 1993.

Garcia, O. & Wei, L. (2014). *Translanguaging: Language, bilingualism, and education*. New York, NY: Palgrave MacMillan.

Harste, J. C., Woodward, V. A., & Burke, C. L. (1984). *Language Stories & Literacy Lessons*. Portsmouth, N.H.: Heinemann.

Kuby, C., Rucker, T.G., & Kirchhofer, J. (2015). 'Go be a writer': Intra-activity with materials, time and space in literacy learning. *Journal of Early Childhood Literacy*, 15(3), 1–26.

Maderazo, C. (2014). The struggle for literacy: Leo's story. In B. Kabuto & P. Martens (Eds.). *Linking families, learning, and schooling: Parent-researcher perspectives* (pp.51-65). New York, NY: Routledge.

Rex, L. (2006). Acting "Cool" and "Appropriate": Toward a framework for considering literacy classroom interactions when race is a factor. *Journal of Literacy Research*, 38(3), 275–325.

Salazar, M.C. (2013). A humanizing pedagogy: Reinventing the principles and practice of education as a journey toward liberation. *Review of Research in Education,* (37), 121-148.

Taylor, D. (1991). *Learning denied*. Portsmouth, NH: Heinemann.

Taylor, D. (1983). *Family literacy: Young children learning to read and write*. Portsmouth, NH: Heinemann.

Negotiating a Permeable Curriculum

On Literacy, Diversity, and the Interplay of Children's and Teachers' Worlds

Anne Haas Dyson

Imagine that it is the end of a long teaching day. You are thumbing through your students' work and come across second grader Eugenie's text (see Figure 1). You sigh and take a closer look at Eugenie's "follow-up" writing to your lesson on the Civil War and Abraham Lincoln. The assignment had been to fold a paper into eight boxes, number each box, and then draw and write in each something important about Lincoln. You hadn't, so far as you can recall, discussed Lincoln's personal life. But here, in Eugenie's paper, is an unidentified woman declaring her love (for Lincoln?) and what you assume to be a marriage scene, "Do you? Yes I do" being a common script among your children for wedding vows. You start to wonder, as teachers often do, if you and Eugenie had participated in the same lesson; if, indeed, you were in the same world.

Figure 1: Eugenie's important facts about Lincoln

This feeling of separation from and puzzling about the lives of children is basic to the topic of this essay: how teachers construct a shared world with their students, or, to rephrase, how they might enact a "permeable" curriculum that allows for interplay between teachers' and children's language and experiences. Such a shared world is essential for the growth of both oral and written language, and it is essential as well if teachers and children are to feel connected to, not alienated from, each other. Indeed, research in schools serving children from diverse sociocultural backgrounds suggests that teachers and children often do feel disconnected, a feeling exacerbated by differences in race and class (Committee on Policy for Racial Justice, 1989; Rothman, 1992).

To counter such alienation, many educators turn to the language arts. For example, we as teachers engage children in literature that reflects the diversity of children's lives and the commonalities of the human spirit, and we encourage children themselves to craft their own experiences, real and imagined, on paper. And yet, whatever curricular materials and activities educators offer, deep in children's own lived worlds, these activities are renegotiated, influenced by social goals which educators might not anticipate and infused with cultural material – thematic content and literacy genres – which they may not value.

Thus, building on what children do – the long-standing truism of both developmentally and culturally appropriate teaching – is not so easy, because doing so involves granting legitimacy and visibility to social purposes and cultural materials that educators may view as trivial, irrelevant, and even distasteful. The permeable curriculum is an idea, like democracy and social justice, that is easy to embrace – until one is faced with the diversity of human values and behaviors, with, for example, a second grader's cryptic text about love, marriage, and Lincoln.

In this essay, I explore the concept of a permeable curriculum, aiming to provide concrete examples of the social and cultural challenges it entails. I draw on a recent study in Eugenie's urban school to illustrate the diverse kinds of social goals that energize young children's language use, particularly their composing, the diverse kinds of cultural material they draw upon, and, most important, the ways in which teachers may work to enact a permeable curriculum, in which the worlds of teachers and children come together in instructionally powerful ways.

Undergirding this essay is a perspective on children and on literacy that differs in emphasis from those most dominant in current pedagogical discussions of the language arts. Informed by the psycholinguistic insights of the seventies and, particularly, by studies of child language development (e.g., Brown, 1973; Read, 1975), pedagogical texts stress that young children are inventors; assisted by others, they figure out how written language works.[1] By engaging in the processes of composing and response, children move beyond egocentric play with writing to true communication.

In contrast, influenced by recent social theories about child language (e.g., Bruner & Haste, 1987; Rogoff, 1990; Stern, 1985), the emphasis herein is on children as social negotiators; addressing others, they explore and exploit the power of symbolic tools as social mediators. The pedagogic goal is not to socialize egocentric child writers but to make varied ways with written language sensible to socially sensitive children, children who live in an increasingly culturally and politically complex society. I introduce this perspective in the following section and then, after two sections featuring the curricular negotiations of Eugenie, her peers, and her teachers, I elaborate on the theoretical substance of the permeable curriculum in the paper's final section.

Dialogue and Development: Children as Social Negotiators

From a sociocultural perspective, the development of language, oral or written, is couched in dialogue. Indeed, words "can only arise in interindividual territory" (Volosinov & Bakhtin, 1973, p. 12), that is, between people who are members of a social unit. Thus, within the interactional rhythms and daily routines of their family lives, young children begin to use language to interpret their experiences. They take words learned from others and use them to give voice to their own feelings and thoughts (Bakhtin, 1986). As Stern (1985) explains:

> Meaning results from interpersonal negotiations involving what can be agreed upon as shared. And such mutually negotiated meanings (the relation of thought to word) grow, change, develop, and are struggled over by two people and thus ultimately owned by us. (p. 170)

Language, therefore, both contributes to and is acquired within common interpretive worlds, in which adults and children share intersubjectivity or "mutually created meanings" about experiences.

On a broader plane, negotiating meanings is also negotiating culture, or the meaning structures shared by people who belong to a particular group (Geertz, 1973). As children grow up in families and communities, they learn ways of interpreting and acting on the world through language. Those culturally patterned ways of using language are evident in stories, jokes, prayers, arguments, and other genres through which people construct their social lives together. The development of language, then, occurs as children learn to participate in ever more effective ways in culturally valued activities mediated through the tool of speech. Children enter into their culture as they tell stories, tease, argue, pray, and, in other ways, interact with others through publicly shared words or other signs (e.g., songs, dramatic actions).

In homes and classrooms, children begin to use written language also as a cultural tool for constructing symbolic worlds and for engaging with others. Young children's written texts are often multimedia affairs, interweavings of written words, spoken ones, and pictures; and yet their graphics, too, can be used as tools within their own worlds, as Eugenie and her peers will illustrate (see also Dyson, 1989; McLane & McNamee, 1990; Newkirk, 1989).

This notion of children entering, through language use, into social and cultural dialogues is complicated in our schools, though, because schools are not homogeneous worlds. Although the teacher governs the official school world, in which children must be students, the children are also members of an unofficial peer world, formed in response to the constraints and regulations of the official world, and they are members as well of their sociocultural communities, which may reform in the classroom amidst networks of peers (D'Amato, 1987; Erickson, 1987; Roberts, 1970). (See Figure 2.)

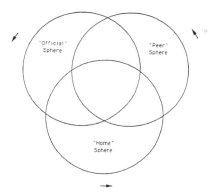

Figure 2. The multiple social worlds of the classroom. (Note: In classrooms, children are at once members of diverse reference spheres. The intention here is not to pull apart that essential dynamic but simply to provide a graphic metaphor of the existence of these spheres. There are no neat boundaries between "home" and "school," nor between the official [teacher-controlled] sphere and that of peers.)

Within each world, children have different kinds of relationships to each other and to their teacher, and, moreover, they enact those relationships through intersecting but nonetheless distinctive ways of using language; that is, each world may have differing notions of effective language use, of appropriate discourse themes, structures, and styles (Hymes, 1980). Thus, teachers offer what they hope will be relevant and intellectually engaging activities, but, within the children's worlds, those activities are interpreted in new ways, infused with unexpected social and cultural meanings.

As teachers, then, we must attend to much more than children's invented words on a page, for writing is not just a specialized way of marking (although it's that, too). Moreover, we cannot assume that our notions of authentic social purposes for writing and response are shared with our young students. Rather, we must attend to children's worlds, for literacy is a way of taking action, of entering into a social dialogue (Bakhtin, 1986; Scribner & Cole, 1981). On the one hand, we must allow – indeed, support – the embedding of written language in children's social worlds, so that they find it a useful symbolic tool (a suggestion made by educators as separated in time and space as Ashton-Warner, Freire, and Vygotsky). But, on the other hand, we must also help children expand and negotiate among the sociocultural worlds – the dialogues – in which they participate.[2] In the words of Rosen and Rosen (1973), a classroom should be

> [a] meeting place of...the children and the adult. The open [permeable] classroom not only welcomes the children and their own ways of thinking and feeling, but it also creates a life of its own...a delicate web of relationships...which is as complicated as that in any home. As complicated but different, for it creates new possibilities, new speculations, new styles. (pp. 31-32)

To illustrate the interplay possible between the worlds of young children and of teachers, I turn to the social and intellectual work done by children and teacher in Eugenie's kindergarten/first-grade classroom, particularly during the daily composing period; the composing period was rich in such interplay, since it was a relatively unstructured time when children were, in fact, supposed to "express themselves" and the teacher was supposed to "respond." Then, to clarify this concept of permeability, I offer an interpretive vision of Eugenie's "Abraham Lincoln" event in a first- and second-grade classroom, an event in which the curriculum was much more impervious to child intrusion.

The Evolution of a Permeable Curriculum

Eugenie's kindergarten/first-grade classroom was in an urban primary (K-3) school in the East San Francisco Bay Area. The school served both an African American community of low-income and working-class households on the southwest side of its attendance area, and an ethnically diverse but primarily European American community of working- to middle-class households on its northeast side.

For two years, I observed in this school, guided by six "key" children, kindergartners through third graders, all African American, who allowed me access to their peers and neighborhood friends. While I focused on children from one sociocultural group in one school, my research concern was not behaviors specific to any one group of children but, rather, the dynamics of, or the interplay between, children's official (teacher-governed) and unofficial (child-governed) classroom worlds and how that interplay figured into children's language use, particularly their composing.[3]

Eugenie's teacher Louise was European American and in her forties; she was an experienced and highly skilled teacher, knowledgeable about recent pedagogical innovations and sensitive to the social issues important to her children. Each day she structured a daily composing period, in which all twenty-seven children drew, wrote, talked, and dictated. After they finished their work, the children gathered on the rug to present their own texts to the classroom audience.

In response to her children, Louise commented on the individual messages and broader genre qualities of their work (i.e., the themes, structures, and styles), and she stressed child reflection and decision making about their texts, as in the following example:

> It's early in October. The children are joining Louise on the rug after a composing period. Louise first notes that Edward J. is making his writing book all about sports. Today he has drawn a boxer and written a backwards "3." The three, Edward then explains, is because "it's the third round."

> Other children, comments Louise, have decided to "label" their pictures. For example, Monique has drawn a tepee and written, "This is me and my TP." Louise comments that hers "could be a picture book."

"A picture book for a little kid," adds a child.

Austin has a twist on the picture book idea. He says that he has made a "guess-what's-happening book." Louise points out that, on the back of each of his pictures, there's a "description of what's happening."

Calvin's is a "wordless picture," featuring a tree, a man, and a hat.

> "What do you think Calvin was thinking of?" Louise asks.
>
> "Caps for Sale," sings the child chorus.
>
> "He doesn't have a mouth," comments a child.
>
> "Does he need a mouth?" Louise asks Calvin.
>
> "No," says Calvin.
>
> "No," says Louise.

As the year progressed, Louise not only used the genre labels of books (e.g., "picture books"); she and the children noted connections of topic, character, plot, and language style (e.g., the use of a rhyming pattern). In this way, she helped children "grow into the intellectual life of those around them" (Vygotsky,

1978, p. 88). Informed by workshops on writing-process pedagogy, she expected that, as the year progressed, the children's desire to communicate and to understand others' texts would lead to their assuming increased responsibility for offering advice to each other as writers (see, for example, Graves, 1983).

But a permeable curriculum – a negotiated classroom culture – cannot emerge from a unidirectional curricular vision. Teachers as well as children must be open, curious, and willing to imagine worlds beyond their own. Louise was such a teacher. In her classroom, the daily meeting time did not progress quite as she had planned. She had, after all, invited the children in as individual decision makers and social actors. And, in time, the children brought their own social goals and, as a result, unanticipated language resources to the daily sharing time.

Their own offerings, and Louise's willingness to respond to those offerings, led to the evolution of what Bruner might call a "cultural forum" (1986, p. 127), in which children's social work and cultural resources and those officially introduced by Louise were connected and expanded in new ways. It was this forum that yielded a dialogic interplay between teachers' and children's worlds and, thus, a permeable curriculum. Before I return to Louise's daily meeting, then, I turn to the children's worlds, where diverse social dialogues occurred as the children took control of the interactional space Louise offered.

Dialogues at Sea: The Social Work of Child Composing

All of the children engaged in a variety of kinds of social work; that is, they established and maintained diverse sorts of relationships with others. Moreover, like adult language-users, they drew upon different genres and different discourse traditions, including those of popular culture and of their sociocultural community. Herein, I aim only to highlight dominant kinds of social work, illustrating children's typical (but not mutually exclusive) ways of making social use of the daily composing time. The categorization or naming of these kinds of social work provides a helpful heuristic for discussing the children's actions, but it is only a heuristic. Children can accomplish varied kinds of social action simultaneously, and they can change social stances quite quickly (as can, of course, adults).

To illustrate their social work and cultural materials, I focus on three child products made during a study unit about oceans, in which Louise and the children talked and read about varied ocean creatures and visited a local aquarium. Fish became a popular topic during this time, as is evidenced by Lamar's "I am a swimmer" piece, Jameel's word-producing fish, and Eugenie's "Callm [clam] lives in here." (See Figures 3, 4, and 5.)

The children, then, had common official curricular experiences to draw upon, and they also were participants in a common official writing "workshop": they were to compose and then share their products, serving as a responsive, helpful audience for each other. And yet, the children enacted very different social dramas as they each took to the sea. Imagine, then, moving to different corners of Louise's classroom as I bring Lamar, Jameel, and Eugenie in focus one by one.

Establishing Social Cohesion: Lamar and Trouble at Sea

Kindergartner Lamar's "I am a swimmer" piece was not energized by an anticipation of rug-time sharing but by composing-time collaborative play. That is, his evolving text was a tool for carrying on a dominant kind of social work in children's as well as adults' worlds – not simply communicating messages but establishing social cohesion, constructing a common world (see Table 1).

Table 1: Samples of Children's Social Work during Composing Time

Sample Text	Dominant Purpose	Text Sense	Addressee Role	Sample Addressee Response
Lamar's sea text	Social cohesion	Shared	Involved collabora-tors or confirmers	"Oh yeah!" "I know"
Jameel's song	Entertain-ing perfor-mance	Humorous/ Artful	Apprecia-tive audi-ence	"That's funny!"

Eugenie's clam text	Commu- nication of informa- tion	Explicit/ Informative	Needy student	"Thank you"

Note: This chart is not intended to be comprehensive. It is intended only to illustrate that words like *audience* and *sense* do not have generic meaning.

To establish cohesive relationships through oral stories, many children drew on material from popular culture – stories about superheroes, verses by rap stars, or scenes from horror movies. Such material was apt to elicit an "Oh yeah, I saw that too" from a child addressee, or a "Me too, I like that too." Sometimes the children jointly recounted the "best parts" of stories from the popular media. "'Member when?" the children would say one after another as episodes were recalled. Sometimes too they engaged in rounds of storytelling, in which they recounted similar (if exaggerated) experiences, as each child outdid the other in the daringness (or silliness) of their actions.

Such responsive interaction was evident in Lamar's early forays into written composing as well, just as it was in his "I am a swimmer" event. In this event, Lamar's collaboration with his good friend James was filtered through each child's separate paper, as it were; but it was collaboration nonetheless, as the following excerpt illustrates. (Note that the ellipses between quotes are indicative of deleted text, and colons within quotes are indicative of elongated pronunciation of the preceding syllable.)

Lamar and James are drawing ocean scenes,

in which they will confront the admired and dreaded shark, sometimes referred to by the boys as "Jaws," after a popular movie featuring a shark. Both boys tell and, sometimes, perform a story as they draw.

James: (chants) I'm swimming in the lake, I'm swimming in the lake. I won't come in and eat my cake.

This gonna be the waves. (drawing waves) This gonna be the waves

...

Lamar: Do you know what these lines are? (pointing to his own drawing [see Figure 3]) They're the waves. They're pushing me this way.

James: Look at these waves (pointing to his own drawing).

Lamar: And then the water gets higher (drawing his waves higher). (Note that "and then" links Lamar's turn with his own previous turn, not with James's.)

James: Mine's gonna get higher, too. My water's higher than you. (Note the use of pronouns ["Mine's"] and repetition ["gonna get higher, too."], both indices of story collaboration [Eder, 1988; Goodwin, 1990])

Lamar: Shoot. Mine is higher than yours

            ...

            Mine is over my head. Told you mine's higher than yours. Mine got deeper. Deeper.

            ...

            (to Tyler) Ain't this deep – ain't this deeper than James's?

Tyler: (nods) It's pretty deep.

James: Look at me diving in the water. Lamar, look at me diving in the water. Look at me diving in the water, Anthony.

            ...

Lamar: And then a shark was coming. Then a shark was coming. (The "and then" links back to Lamar's previous storylines.)

            ...

James: If they had a shark in the water, we'd get ready to get out of the water.

Lamar: I'm getting ready to get out of the water 'cause the shark. (Lamar takes James's idea and incorporates it into his own story.)

            ...

            (chanting) I'm deep in the water. The shark's gonna kill me.

James: But oh ! There's a shark in the water. (Now James incorporates Lamar's idea into his own story. The "But oh !" refers to a development in James's own piece.)

          …

Lamar: I'm gonna make the blood coming out 'cause the shark bit the octopus. I'm gonna make the blood in the water. (adds red by octopus)

Later, with the help of Mrs. Johnson, a teaching assistant, both boys write "I am a swimmer."

Figure 3: Lamar's adventure at sea

The social meaning of Lamar's multimedia story (woven from talking, drawing, and writing) was

linked to that of James's. The children declared themselves as vulnerable but brave – or "braver than you"
– boys in a world of monsters. Each text was motivated by, and contributed to, the boys' relationship
as best friends.

Taking the Spotlight: Jameel and the Singing Fish.

Although Lamar's efforts were energized by his
ongoing play with James, first grader Jameel's crafting
of his fish text was fueled by the anticipation of rug-
time sharing. But he did not eagerly await communication with helpful peers; he anticipated an artful
performance for an appreciative, admiring audience
(see Table 1). He brooked no advice from others when
his moment in the spotlight finally arrived.

Although Jameel was the most consistent performer in his class, all of the observed children
engaged in performances. In doing so, they often
drew on their oral folk resources (i.e., the features of
verbal art, which highlight the musical and image-
creating properties of language [Bauman, 1986; Smitherman, 1986; Tannen, 1989]), and they also tended
to explicitly manipulate their texts; for example,
they tried to make words rhyme, phrases rhythmic,
dialogue fast-paced, and images funny. The aim was
not a confirming "me, too" but a pleased and perhaps
surprised "Oh!" or even laughter.

To compose his singing fish, Jameel combined his

interest in rhythmic, poetic, humorous prose with an interest in scientific exposition, and he brought together his enjoyment of popular cartoons with his fascination with the ocean study unit.

Jameel: [I wrote it] 'cause I love singing. Then I started loving animals. And then I thought, "I'll make 'em singing a song. A singing fish."

As seen in Figure 4, on the top of his paper, Jameel had drawn a fish with four large bubbles coming out of its mouth. These are both comic-like and air bubbles – a visual pun. In each bubble is a "tune," that is, the words being sung by the fish. (The words of the song had, in fact, come from comic-like and surreptitious operatic singing ["me me me" and "my my my"] many children, including Jameel, had been doing during morning singing.)

The bottom half of the page is an exposition of the fish, written in a performative style, with paired, contrastive variants of a sentence. The voice on the bottom text is an "announcer," as Jameel explained. Moreover, Jameel had made a stapled pocket on the bottom of his song. This, he said, was for the money donations that would surely follow when he took his singing fish to the streets.

Jameel: [People will] pay money for it, the fish. But it's gonna be me [taking the money]. And I'm only give the fish a itsy bitsy piece of candy. And I'm gonna keep the money.

However, the streets of most immediate concern were those of his classroom neighborhood. As he worked, Jameel did not want to sing his song to any of his neighbors, so to speak; they would have to wait for the appropriate time, that is, for show time on the rug.

Figure 4: Jameel's singing fish: "That fish isn't any ordinary fish. It's a singing fish."

Helping a Needy Colleague: Eugenie and the Clam in the Shell

Lamar's and Jameel's peer Eugenie, a first grader, displayed two different kinds of social work as she composed her ocean piece. One sort of work is similar to that displayed by Lamar, since it involves social cohesion. But it does not necessarily involve collaboratively producing a text. Rather, it involves collegially acknowledging peers as people in the same boat, as it were. That is, the children commiserated about the trials and tribulations of learning to write, including spelling and spacing, doing it over and trying to read it. Listen, for example, to Eugenie's reaction to Shawnda's lament (colons in text are indicative of an elongated sound or syllable):

"Shucks," said Shawnda. "I erased that whole row [of writing] and I'm doing it over. (Eugenie giggles.) I don't care if it is recess time. I'm gonna do it over and I might do it over 10,000 times. I mean that."

"O::, I know how you feel, gir::l!" responded Eugenie with great conviction. "I KNOW, HOW, YOU, FEEL!"

The children valued informal, mutual helping. Colleagues help each other and do not expose each other's weaknesses in public places. Still, when the opportunity presented itself, Eugenie, like all the observed children, took the opportunity to teach a needy other, often using, at least in part, Louise's straightforward style and professional vocabulary. To accomplish this other kind of social work (see Table 1), Eugenie, as teacher, required a student, preferably a grateful one, and she found Vera a willing learner in the "clam" event. In the following excerpt, note how Eugenie presents a collegial "we" to Mrs. Johnson, despite her adoption of a leadership role with Vera.

Figure 5 presents Eugenie's completed text.

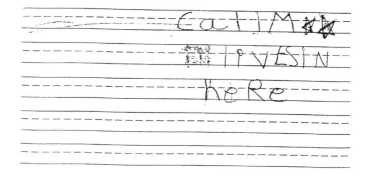

Figure 5: Eugenie's hypothesized clam shell

Eugenie and Vera have taken a shell from a large basket in the classroom. They are each going to write about what might have lived in that shell.

Vera: Now what does live in this shell?

               …

Eugenie: This is not fact. This is fiction. (Note the use of the school terms "fact" and "fiction.")

               …

               Do you think a clam might be living in here? See, like a clam might be living in here. But he left his color of this spot to let us know. It might be a little clam. (Note how Eugenie puts forth a hypothetical statement and links that statement to a previous observation [that the shell had a brown spot].)

Vera: That's true

               ….

Eugenie: Mrs. Johnson, come here. Me and Vera made a decision. We thought that a clam might live in the shell. (Note the explicit reference to making "a decision"; such reference was common in Louise's talk to children but not common in the children's unofficial talk.)

Performers, colleagues, collaborators, teachers, and students – Lamar, Jameel, and Eugenie were complex social actors in classroom worlds, and these ends influenced their ways of enacting, participating in, classroom literacy events. They drew upon diverse sorts of cultural materials as they worked toward varied ends.

A Cultural Forum in Action

The children, with their diverse social roles and resources, did not fit neatly into the social order Louise originally had imagined. She had, for example, suggested an opening ten minutes of "quiet writing time," but her children talked. Moreover, Louise had anticipated children corning to the rug to communicate to a peer "audience" which would offer comments and suggestions. But the desire to communicate per se was not necessarily the children's dominant goal – indeed, sometimes the major goal was achieved before they arrived at the rug (as with Lamar's collaborative work with James). Further, the children objected to an advice-giving audience, a role, after all, that differs substantively from that of editor or formal critic in our common culture (for elaboration of this point, see Dyson, 1992, 1993).

Nor was it so easy for Louise to figure out what advice she should give about content. Most pedagogical suggestions for young children assume making a better, more sensible text has to do with making ideas more explicit (i.e., writing less "egocentrically"). But the crafting of the singing fish text, for example, did not have to do with explicitness but with rhythm.

The children were exploring the ways in which they might act on and in their worlds through the written medium. In response, Louise, first, allowed continued space for what the children were doing; after all, colleagues must be free to consult and commiserate, to admire and admonish – and to find a space apart for private shaping and reflection. Similarly, collaborators require partners, performers need an audience, and "teachers" must have "students," or they cannot enact their roles, display their skills, or accomplish the ends that make their lives satisfying. Louise sometimes explicitly and officially acknowledged that social work. For example, she talked with her children about their preferred ways of composing, making explicit the variation and offering choices. Did they wish to write alone? With a partner? In a quiet corner? On a table with other composers?

Second, Louise took advantage of the diversity of cultural material the children brought to the rug. In the presented examples, the genres included horror stories and pop songs, but they could have been cartoons or raps, "true stories" filled with hyperbole, or expressive "love stories".[4] In response to the children's inclusiveness, Louise worked to help children name their efforts, to place their work in the social landscape of discourse.

To do this, Louise provided children's texts with the dignity of a name (e.g., fiction, nonfiction, descriptions, songs, games, poems, jokes), a practice the children gradually engaged in as well. And she worked to establish connections between their efforts and that of the wider world of discourse. For example, when Lamar brought his "shark" piece to the meeting on the rug, he explained to the class about the shark, the octopus, and his own precarious presence in the water; in turn, Louise helped his piece become part of general class reflection on fish stories that were mainly factual and those that were mainly fictional. (Louise herself introduced the term "whale of a tale.") Eugenie's piece fed into the cultural forum in similar ways, although, unlike Lamar, Eugenie made sure the class knew that she and Vera had worked on the same shell (a point made in part to irritate Vera's friend Shawnda, with whom Eugenie herself had a rather tenuous relationship).

Jameel's piece fed into the class forum in a particularly dramatic way, and therefore the interplay between Jameel's social intentions and Louise's response is particularly revealing. Jameel had come to the rug specifically to entertain the class – and he did so. Sitting on the rug during sharing time, Jameel sang his song for his classmates in a crooning voice, like Bing Crosby or Nat King Cole. His singing is presented in phrase groups, with hyphens indicative of a careful pronunciation of the letter itself. (Note that colons are indicative of elongated pronunciation of the preceding syllable.)

Jameel: M-Y-M-Y: (sings each letter in a smooth, rising tune, elongating the last Y; he has

Jameel: written periods after each letter [e.g.,

M.Y.M.Y.] to indicate that each is to be sung separately.)

M-Y-M-Y: (sings similarly)

M:-M: (continues on the high pitch with elongated Ms)

me me me: (even pitch)

you you you: (even but higher pitch)

my my my: (even but higher pitch)

M-Y-M-Y: (as before)

I: lo::ve (elongated and with a rhythmic drop and then rise in pitch)

you, to, boop boo bee do (syncopated)

M-Y-M-Y: (as before)

That fish isn't any ordinary fish. It's a singing fish. (reads in an announcer's voice; note the repetition and variation in sentence structure)

Jameel's song received much applause and laughter. It was, in short, a hit. In the afternoon following his morning performance, many of his classmates decided to write songs themselves.

Louise responded to the songs by incorporating them and their participation framework (i.e., the performer and audience roles) into the official classroom world. As was Louise's strategy, she used professional language to establish links between the children's songs and those of the wider world and, just as importantly, to provide tools for reflection. She explained the necessity of taping their tunes; without special writing skills, taping would be the only way that those tunes could be remembered. She brainstormed with the children about other books they had read that contained tunes whose graphic features they could study, and she consulted with the school music teacher, who talked to the children about how music was written. Perhaps this respectful and serious response (filled, as it was, with good fun) contributed to Jameel's increased reflectiveness about his songwriting (e.g., purposefully checking his songs before performances, adjusting lines that didn't "work," that is, sound right to his ear).

Louise's response to Jameel's songs is indicative of the larger interplay among cultural material in her classroom. The children studied the local symphony and local rappers; they read folktales of varied peoples and children's books written in diverse vernaculars. Each child's own composed text thus entered into an intertextual universe – a school culture – that was not some kind of anemic world, where words are disembedded from social contexts (cf. Donaldson, 1978); it was one where words reverberated with the diverse rhythms and sounds of human voices. And, of course, one to which the children contributed. Thus, the enacted curriculum in Louise's classroom included a diversity of texts, of kinds of sense, and of possible dialogic responses to children's oral and written words.

From Permeable Curricular Main Roads to Limiting Side Roads

To clarify this concept of the permeable curriculum – this interplay between children's and adults' worlds – I consider events of one year later. Eugenie was then in the second grade and in another classroom, one in which interactive space and academic demands were more clearly specified, as, in fact, is a typical change in classrooms as children move through school (Goodlad, 1984).

The "follow-up activity" to the Lincoln lesson was illustrative – the children were to fold their paper into eight boxes, unfold them, and then draw and write a fact about Lincoln in each box. In many similar activities, sample sentences were put on the board. While the children did not orally present their work, it was regularly "published;" that is, the work was bound in class-made books or displayed on bulletin boards.

The activities in which Eugenie and her peers engaged were commonplace. Her teacher was hardworking and caring, not an out-of-touch educator who passed out dittos and basal readers. But the very typical nature of the activities – and the ways in which they were enacted within the children's social worlds – made the classroom an invaluable setting for applying and, thereby clarifying, the concept of permeability.

To reiterate, the aim herein is not to make generalizations about particular teachers or teaching practices but, through examining such particulars, to illuminate an idea – permeability – that might help educators in other situations "ferret out the unapparent import of things" (Geertz, 1973, p. 126), things like a child's text about Lincoln and love.

Historical Facts or Fiction: Eugenie and Mr. Lincoln

As Eugenie set to work on the Lincoln piece, she looked up from time to time at her two friends in the second grade, Vanessa and LaToya. (The friends' desks were strategically separated by her teacher.)

Eugenie began by drawing Lincoln wearing a tall hat, but her drawing was interrupted by a loud whisper from Vanessa, who was holding up her picture. Vanessa was hard to hear, but she clearly had drawn Abraham Lincoln getting shot at a theater. Eugenie quickly wrote "He was nice" under her first picture and began work on her own theater picture. She drew a girl with long blond hair – Lincoln's child, she said, or maybe "a friend of his." (She wasn't sure if Lincoln had any kids or not.) Nonetheless, Eugenie had a dramatic scene in mind, one centered on what might have happened before that fateful trip to the theater:

Figure 6: Vanessa's important facts about Lincoln

Eugenie: (presenting her work to me) She's
             [the drawn girl] saying, "I love you."
             Because before he got ready to go
             to the theater, she said, "Even if you
             get killed, I still love you." (said with
             great feeling)

Eugenie wrote "I Love You" in a bubble coming
out of the girl's mouth. Then, with a glance at her
teacher (in the corner with a child), she moved over
to Vanessa's desk. LaToya soon followed. Vanessa
presented her completed paper to her two friends
(see Figure 6).

She had not focused on Lincoln's political life, the
emphasis of the lesson, but on his personal life. While
lacking in precise details, she had drawn Lincoln as a

little boy by a house, Lincoln as a man by yet another house, Lincoln's girlfriend, Lincoln getting married (complete with wedding vows), and the house where Lincoln and his wife lived. Interspersed with Vanessa's presentation of her work, the children discussed their own views on boyfriends (they currently did not have them), growing up (much anticipated), and babies (they all wanted them).

Mrs. Walker, the classroom teaching assistant, who had just entered the room from another classroom, sent the girls back to their seats. Back in her own place again, Eugenie drew Lincoln's house, his wife, and his wedding day (complete with vows). (See Figure 1; final three pictures completed at another time.)

Eventually, Vanessa and LaToya came to Eugenie's desk. Eugenie now presented her work to her friends, dramatically reading the line "I love you" and explaining its import. LaToya then motioned her friends into the classroom library; she had a dance step to show them. Her teacher saw the dancing and sent them back to their seats.

During this event, Eugenie's stance was primarily a collegial, at times collaborative, one. She discussed her decisions and textual content with her friends. Moreover, Eugenie's written voice was influenced by the social work she engaged in with her friends; her piece on Lincoln reflected the themes and dramatic style of the girls' talk among themselves. Eugenie had, in effect, composed an official school text by drawing on unofficial worlds. But that text did not function as a kind of crossroad among worlds.

There was no public forum for Eugenie to present her work in the official world, to bring out her performative language, the dramatized event she had imagined, the family life she had constructed when drawing. Without a forum, there was also no way to socially analyze the work (for example, the decision to imagine details), to compare it to other classmates' decisions, or to connect it with varied kinds of genres in the larger world (e.g., historical fiction, melodramas or child "love stories"). Her unofficial social and language work could not become part of the official classroom culture. Her text would be checked for completion according to the required assignment – paper folded into eight boxes, eight pictures and eight sentences about Lincoln's life, all nongenre-related criteria. In the official world, her "I do's" and "I love you" became textual equivalents to dancing in the library, behaviors clearly off the curricular main road.

Thus, Eugenie's social and language resources did not enter into the larger classroom community, nor, for that matter, did the language of the larger community enter in a substantive way into Eugenie's collegial talk and composing. Eugenie was not making decisions about potential kinds of literacy dialogues ("This is not fact. This is fiction."). She had composed along a curricular side road, one with limited possibility of connecting up with the main road.

Reflections on the Permeable Curriculum: Theoretical Themes

This essay began with an image of a teacher puzzling over Eugenie's piece about Mr. Lincoln. The teacher felt unconnected to the life world of her student, at a loss in her efforts to understand where Eugenie was coming from. This image is reflective of the feelings of many teachers about their students – and of the feelings of many students about their teachers (Rothman, 1992). Indeed, by the middle school years, the life worlds of school and those of peers and communities are often rigidly separated in the minds of students (Sleeter & Grant, 1991).

The intention herein is not to devalue the social and cultural materials of the official curriculum. But it is to suggest that those materials are of no use unless they engage children with the social and cultural worlds they know best and, moreover, to suggest that both child worlds and school worlds would be considerably enriched by the interplay made possible in a permeable curriculum. Such a curriculum seeks to acknowledge and respect the complexity of children's social worlds and cultural materials. And it attempts, not only to create bridges between worlds, but to support children's own naming and manipulating of the dynamic relationships among worlds. That is, it aims to help children understand and negotiate among multiple social worlds by means of diverse ways with words (Hymes, 1980). In complex modern societies, it is negotiating among – "managing" (Hymes, 1980, p. 45) – diverse ways with words that is the essential discourse challenge.

By highlighting the experiences of the children in Eugenie's school, I hoped to provide concrete examples of such permeability, of what respect for children's social worlds, and for their cultural materials, might look like, and of how a cultural forum might help both children's and teachers' worlds expand. Just as important, I hoped to illustrate the theoretical ideas about literacy, particularly composing, about cultural diversity, and about teaching that undergird such an evolving curriculum. Next, I highlight three key ideas and their implications for the permeable curriculum.

Composing as Social Dialogue

From the perspective of this essay, composing is always a situated response, an addressing of another in a particular time and place, a motivated making of words for some end. That is, written words are only mediators and, for young children especially, only partial mediators of social action. Approaching children's texts as social action, then, requires sensitivity to the logic of children's own social worlds. And those worlds, in turn, require interactive space in our classrooms. In the intimate worlds children construct together, they use a range of cultural resources to enact roles as colleagues and collaborators, performers and audience members, teachers and, of course, students.

Moreover, making use of children's social intelligence entails rethinking the generic nature of writing pedagogy for young children. Teachers are encouraged to arrange social situations in which child composers receive "responses" to their texts from "authentic" audiences of peers. But a teacher's quiet writing time might be a child's collaborative work period; a teacher's "whole-group writing" conference might be a child's show-time stage; and a teacher's occasion for peer editing might be viewed by the children as an occasion for collegiality. Considering children as social actors thus suggests that "audience," "editor," and "response" are situated, not generic, terms that can be explicitly discussed and planned for with children. And it suggests as well the importance of diverse situations for composing – and diverse text types.

To elaborate, pedagogical writing about child literacy often assumes that the developmental goal is "decontextualized" written language (e.g., Olson, 1984), that is, language in which ideas are made explicit in tightly constructed prose, rather than implicitly understood by familiar interlocutors. But, given that written language always exists within a kind of social relationship, so-called "decontextualized" language also exists only in certain situational and text contexts, that is, in certain genres. Moreover, children can begin writing by producing a diversity of genres – and any one child may control diverse sorts of texts. Official recognition of diverse types or genres, though, necessitates a dialogic perspective, not simply toward literacy, but toward cultural traditions themselves.

A Dialogic Perspective on Cultural Traditions

As social actors, young children draw on a diversity of cultural materials. The easy ways in which they move among cultural traditions, creating stories that blend folk, popular, and written traditions, reflect, in fact, the complex, dialogic relationships that link traditions. For example, the daily rhythms of music and talk that arise from the regional and ethnic cultures of our society – from the "folk" – have transformed both "popular" and "high" culture (Gates, 1989). In addition, popular cultural forms can express an oppositional attitude – a distancing, a playfulness – to the "high," the serious, the "towering" (Bakhtin, 1981), which may account for their appeal to the young.

However, most discussions of young children as literacy users draw firm lines between the literacy experiences of children who have had extended preschool exposure to children's literature and, particularly, storybooks, and of those who have not had such experiences. Through reading and talking about books, parents introduce children to the explicit or "decontextualized" prose valued in school. And yet, children's literature draws on a diversity of cultural genres, including jazz tunes and folk songs, cartoons and oral lore, as well as the wealth of spoken English vernaculars (Kushkin, 1980). Moreover, cultural labels are themselves quite fuzzy; for example, in nineteenth-century America, "popular culture" – the cultural art forms meaningful to diverse regional, class, and ethnic groups – included Shakespeare, opera, and classical music, along with juggling, parodies, and songs (Levine, 1988).

Recently, scholars working with older students have emphasized how the rhetorical features of peer and folk ways with words (e.g., oral stories and language plays, metaphors and insult games) are potentially powerful learning and language tools across the curriculum. And they have written about their efforts to help students make deliberate use of their range of discourse strategies in both literary and academic writing (Ball, 1992; Redd, 1992; Scott, 1990; Smitherman, 1986, 1994). We who work in early childhood and elementary education can contribute to such efforts by broadening our vision of the kinds of cultural resources that support literacy growth.

Perhaps there is a fear of acknowledging and building upon diverse discourse themes, genre structures, and styles, because of our human propensity toward dichotomous thinking. As educators, we have categorized children as "at-risk" or not, "mainstream" or "nonmainstream," and we have associated certain categories – and the possibility of school success – exclusively with certain ways of using language. More broadly, as a society, we have used speech styles and art forms as ways of gauging intellectual and aesthetic superiority and inferiority, of reinforcing boundaries of class, ethnicity, and culture (Hymes, 1980; Levine,

1988).

But language in use is inherently diverse – changing with situation, role, and activity – and humans are remarkably flexible language users; given a reason (and opportunities for practice), we are code-switchers, register collectors, and players with speech (Garvey, 1990; Gilyard, 1991; Labov, 1969). There is no reason to assume that a child who writes pop songs for a singing fish cannot deliver a lecture on the nature of ocean creatures – certainly Jameel could (particularly when given an opportunity to teach; for examples, see Dyson, 1992, 1993). Nor, of course, is there a reason to think that an effective lecture can be given in only one style (Farr, 1993). To repeat, the essential language skill is not mastery of any one genre or style – it is the capacity to negotiate among contexts, to be socially and politically astute in discourse use.

Further, while there is ample reason for adult concern about the sometimes sexist, racist, and violent images of the popular media, children's literature is not immune from such charges (Gilbert, 1989; Sims, 1982). Moreover, lack of acknowledgement of many young students' deep fascination with the popular media does not help them develop a critical perspective.

The acknowledgement of human and language complexity seems to be a critical first step in respectful relationships between teachers and students and in the building of a shared life, which leads to the final idea that undergirds the permeable curriculum, that of a cultural forum.

Curiosity, Respect, and the Cultural Forum

Like us all, children negotiate membership in overlapping, sometimes contradictory, worlds governed by "imaginative universes" – cultures, as it were, or shared ways of infusing objects and actions with meaning (Geertz, 1973). But, as teachers, we only have access to parts of children's selves. Respect for the diversity of children's worlds and for the partiality of our own visions keeps us from putting children into neat "sociological categories of race, social class, ethnicity and family structure [which then] become the primary factors of differentiating among children" (Lightfoot, 1978, p. 211). Respect also fuels our interest in children's lives, our desire as teachers to understand the factors that contribute to a child's wholeness, to their individuality.

Teachers with such curiosity talk with (not simply about) parents and community members, seeking insight into children's lives beyond the school walls and into the language use that pervades those lives (for suggestions about such talk, see Barr et al., 1988). Moreover, they invite children themselves to share responsibility for negotiating the language life – the valued texts – of classroom life (Genishi, 1992). In this way the negotiated culture of the classroom is enriched, as diverse genres, diverse cultural traditions, mingle on the classroom stage, giving rise to "new possibilities, new speculations, new styles" (Rosen & Rosen, 1973, p. 32).

Critical to such negotiation is an ongoing cultural forum. I am not referring to a "whole-class conference," the main purpose of which is to support the development of individual children's writing. Rather, I am suggesting a forum, within which children might explain about Lincoln and imagined loves, about Jaws in the deep and decisions about clams, and within which we as educators connect their efforts with the world beyond. And, at the same time, it is a forum in which our own world view is enriched by those of the children.

In Closing: Behind the Curricular Curtain

In *The Woman Warrior*, Maxine Hong Kingston (1977) writes about the puzzlement and alarm her elementary school teachers expressed about her school paintings.

"I painted layers of black over houses and flowers and suns," she wrote, "and when I drew on the blackboard, I put a layer of chalk on top" (p. 192). Her teachers consulted with her parents rather than with the silent Maxine, but her parents did not speak English. What no one, parents or teachers, knew was that Maxine "was making a stage curtain, and it was the moment before the curtain parted or rose." When her parents took her pictures home, Maxine "spread them out (so black and full of possibilities) and pretended the curtains were swinging open, flying up, one after another, sunlight underneath, mighty operas."

In a similar way, dramas unfold behind the curtain of the official curriculum. Those dramas, like the ones of Hong Kingston's imagination, are the stuff of children's lives (indeed, they are the stuff of our own memories of childhood) – dramas of friends and fights, of imagined melodramas and high adventures, and, in fact, of the thrill of being behind the curtain, protected in some way from the judgments and orders of the adult world. Still, if we are to teach the children, we have to tap into these child worlds, and we have to offer them tools – ways of thinking and talking – that will help them negotiate their way into a future of possibilities.

In a troubled world of poverty and violence, of racism and sometimes breathtaking indifference, we cannot pave children's way. But, as teachers, we can help. Within our classrooms, children compose texts that declare their existence in the world, but that existence is acknowledged, momentarily completed, only by the response of the other (Bakhtin, 1986). In our own responses to the children, we help shape their understanding of what it means to be an educated person in our society. If our classrooms are not places for a diversity of social action and a wealth of cultural materials, we risk sending messages of alienation, messages that say that educated people are not rooted in their own histories, in strong relationships with people that matter.

Moreover, we deny them, and ourselves, the scholarly benefit – and the good fun – possible when language and experiences are shared. For, in answering the children, we are also composing ourselves. In their plurality, in their diversity, our children offer us the opportunity to open wider the curtains framing our own world view, so that we might see aspects of experience that otherwise would remain invisible to us, so that we might better understand ourselves as situated in a complex world of multiple perspectives (Greene, 1988).

Eugenie's piece on Lincoln and love, for example, set me wondering about the story of the Civil War and about history itself as it was taught to me, that is, as a series of wars. I wondered what a little girl like Eugenie (or like the once-me), so attuned to relationships, could identify with in such a story – what would tap her experiences and feelings, what would feed into her social talk with friends. I thought about why she and her friends had snuck around behind the curricular curtain, situating Lincoln in the themes of their own play. And I wondered about how the children's fascination with Lincoln and his loves connected with the political stories of relationships (sanctioned and not) that pervade our political campaigns. I reflected on how history (including war) becomes a dehumanized topic, on how humanized history attracts so many of us (as did the PBS special on the Civil War).

I wondered and wandered far from Eugenie, Lincoln, and the second grade, and then returned again to underscore, as I do now, the complexity of social work and intellectual thought that are revealed when we push back the curricular curtains. Children's texts are sites for negotiation among multiple social worlds, worlds energized by dreams and fears, friendships and kinships. In working to create a permeable curriculum, we bring at least some of the energy of these worlds into the official classroom world and, in so doing, we enrich the cultural conversations of us all.

Notes

1. Temple, Nathan, Temple, and Burris (1993) is a thorough text (now in its third edition) that, in emphasis, represents well dominant perspectives. The first chapter begins with an example of invented spelling. Although the importance of adult modeling is emphasized, the child is characterized as egocentric, with reference to Piaget, and learning to write is presented primarily as an act of discovery.

2. For an illuminating autobiographical portrayal of a child's negotiation among worlds, see Gilyard, 1991.

3. To elaborate, I was interested in the contextual specifics of children's discourse use. I wondered how children used varied kinds of language art forms and cultural traditions (e.g., those of their ethnic communities, of popular culture, of shared classroom literature) as they

interacted with teachers and peers throughout the school day, that is, as they engaged in social work through oral and written language. (For discussions of the ethnography of communication, the traditions of which guided this work, see Gumperz & Hymes, 1986; for details of data collection and analysis, see Dyson, 1993.)

4. "True stories" was a term used by the children. It referred to exaggerated stories with elements of truth in them (for discussions of the role of such stories in African American culture, see Smitherman, 1986, and Heath, 1983, who uses the same emic term). "Love stories" was also a child term, introduced by Jameel, to refer to texts composed of questions and statements about classmates' special friends.

References

Bakhtin, M. (1981). Discourse in the novel. In C. Emerson & M. Holquist (Eds.), *The dialogic imagination: Four essays by M. Bakhtin* (pp.259-422). Austin, TX: University of Texas Press.

Bakhtin, M. (1986). *Speech genres and other late essays*. Austin, TX: University of Texas Press.

Ball, A. (1992). Cultural preference and the expository writing of African-American adolescents. *Written Communication*, 9, 501-532.

Barr, M., Ellis, S., Hester, H., & Thomas, A. (1988). *The primary language record*. Portsmouth, NH: Heinemann.

Bauman, R. (1986). *Story, performance, and event: Contextual studies of oral narrative*. Cambridge, NY: Cambridge University Press.

Brown, R. (1973). *A first language: The early stages*. Cambridge, MA: Harvard University Press.

Bruner, J. (1986). *Actual minds, possible worlds*. Cambridge, MA: Harvard University Press.

Bruner, J., & Haste, H. (Eds.). (1987). *Making sense: The child's construction of the world*. New York, NY: Methuen.

Committee on Policy for Racial Justice. (1989). *Visions of a better way: A Black appraisal of public schooling*. Washington, DC: Joint Center for Political Studies Press.

D'Amato, J. D. (1987). The belly of the beast: On cultural difference, castelike status, and the politics of school. *Anthropology & Education Quarterly*, 18, 357-360.

Donaldson, M. (1978). *Children's minds*. New York, NY: Norton.

Dyson, A. H. (1989). *Multiple worlds of child writers: Friends learning to write*. New York, NY: Teachers

College Press.

Dyson, A. H. (1992). The case of the singing scientist: A performance perspective on the "stages" of school literacy. *Written Communication, 9*, 3-47.

Dyson, A.H. (1993). *The social worlds of children learning to write in an urban primary school.* New York, NY: Teachers College Press.

Eder, D. (1988). Building cohesion through collaborative narration. *Social Problems Quarterly, 51*, 225-235.

Erickson, F. (1987). Transformation and school success: The politics and culture of educational achievement. *Anthropology & Education Quarterly, 18*, 335-356.

Farr, M. (1993). Essayist literacy and other verbal performances. *Written Communication, 10*, 4-38.

Garvey, C. (1990). *Play* (enlarged edition). Cambridge, MA: Harvard University Press.

Gates, H. L., Jr. (1989). Canon-formation, literary history, and the Afro-American tradition: From the seen to the told. In H. A. Baker, Jr. & P. Redmond (Eds.), *Afro-American literary study in the 1990s* (pp. 14-38). Chicago: The University of Chicago Press.

Geertz, C. (1973). *The interpretation of cultures:*

Selected essays. New York, NY: Basic Books.

Genishi, C. (Ed.). (1992). *Ways of assessing children and curriculum: Stories of early childhood practice*. New York, NY: Teachers College Press.

Gilbert, P. (1989). *Gender, literacy, and the classroom*. Carlton South, Victoria: Australian Reading Association.

Gilyard, K. (1991). *Voices of the self: A study of language competence*. Detroit, MI: Wayne State University Press.

Goodlad, J. (1984). *A place called school: Prospects for the future*. New York, NY: McGraw-Hill.

Goodwin, M. (1990). *He-said-she-said: Talk as social organization among black children*. Bloomington, IN: Indiana University Press.

Graves, D. H. (1983). *Writing: Teachers and children at work*. Portsmouth, NH: Heinemann Educational Books.

Greene, M. (1988). *The dialectic of freedom*. New York, NY: Teachers College Press.

Gumperz, J., & Hymes, D. (Eds.). (1986). *Directions in sociolinguistics: The ethnography of communication* (2nd ed.). New York, NY: Basil Blackwell.

Hymes, D. (1980). *Language in education*. Washington, DC: Center for Applied Linguistics.

Kingston, M. H. (1977). *The woman warrior*. New York, NY: Random House.

Kushkin, K. (1980). The language of children's literature. In L. Michaels & C. Ricks (Eds.), *The state of the language* (pp. 213-225). Berkeley, CA: University of California Press.

Labov, W. (1969). The logic of nonstandard English. In J. E. Alatis (Ed.), *Report of the twentieth annual roundtable meeting on linguistics and language study* (pp. 1-44). Washington, DC: Georgetown University Press.

Levine, L. (1988). *Highbrow/lowbrow: The emergence of cultural hierarchy in America*. Cambridge, MA: Harvard University Press.

Lightfoot, S. (1978). *Worlds apart: Relationships between families and schools*. New York, NY: Basic Books.

McLane, J. & McNamee, G. (1990). *Early literacy*. Cambridge, MA: Harvard University Press.

Newkirk, T. (1989). *More than stories: The range of children's writing*. Portsmouth, NH: Heinemann.

Olson, D. (1984). "See! Jumping!" Some oral antecedents of literacy. In H. Goelman, A. Oberg, & F. Smith (Eds.), *Awakening to literacy* (pp. 185-192).

Portsmouth, NH: Heinemann.

Read, C. (1975). *Children's categorization of speech sounds in English*. Urbana, IL: National Council of Teachers of English.

Redd, T. (1992). "Styling" in black students' writing for black audiences. Paper presented at the meeting of the American Educational Research Association, San Francisco, CA.

Roberts, J. (1970). *Scene of the battle: Group behavior in urban classrooms*. Garden City, NY: Doubleday.

Rogoff, B. (1990). *Apprenticeship in thinking: Cognitive development in social context*. New York, NY: Oxford University Press.

Rosen, C., & Rosen, H. (1973). *The language of primary school children*. Harmondsworth, Middlesex, England: Penguin.

Rothman, R. (1992, December). Study from "inside" finds a deeper set of school problems. *Education Week*, 12 (13), pp. 1, 9.

Scott, J. C. (1990). The silent sounds of language variation in the classroom. In S. Hynds & D. Rubin (Eds.), *Perspectives on talk and learning* (pp. 285-298). Urbana, IL: National Council of Teachers of English.

Scribner, S., & Cole, M. (1981). *The psychology of lit-*

eracy. Cambridge, MA: Harvard University Press.

Sims, R. (1982). *Substance and shadow: Afro-American experience in contemporary children's literature*. Urbana, IL: National Council of Teachers of English.

Sleeter, C., & Grant, C. (1991). Mapping terrains of power: Student cultural knowledge versus classroom knowledge. In C. Sleeter (Ed.), *Empowerment through multi-cultural education* (pp. 49-68). Albany: State University of New York Press.

Smitherman, G. (1986). *Talkin and testifyin: The language of Black America*. Detroit: Wayne State University Press.

Smitherman, G. (1994). "The blacker the berry, the sweeter the juice": African American student writers and the national assessment of educational progress. In A. H. Dyson & C. Genishi (Eds.), *The need for story: Cultural diversity in classroom and community*. Urbana, IL: National Council of Teachers of English.

Stern, D. (1985). *The interpersonal world of the infant: A view from psychoanalysis and developmental psychology*. New York, NY: Basic Books.

Tannen, D. (1989). *Talking voices: Repetition, dialogue, and imagery in conversational discourse*. Cambridge, NY: Cambridge University Press.

Temple, C., Nathan, R., Temple, F., & Burris, N. (1993). *The beginnings of writing*. Needham Heights, MA: Allyn & Bacon.

Volosinov, V. N., & Bakhtin, M. (1973). *Marxism and the philosophy of language* (L. Matejka & I. R. Titunik, Trans.). New York, NY: Seminar Press.

Vygotsky, L. (1978). *Mind in society*. Cambridge, MA: Harvard University Press.

An Interview with Anne Haas Dyson

Bobbie: You have been researching and writing about children's writing since 1981when you published your first article in *Language Arts* titled *Oral language: The rooting system for learning to write*. You are a prolific writer! Since that first article, you have published 12 books and over 100 journal articles and book chapters all regarding children's writing, or what you have learned from observing and researching children's writing. Can you talk a little about how you became interested in children's writing?

Anne: I became incredibly interested in children's writing when I started teaching in El Paso in the early seventies. When I gave my 6- to 8-year olds a piece of paper and a request that they write, I was amazed at the differences in how the children responded. My children, all without economic advantages but with the gift of bilingualism, responded in all sorts of ways.

One little one made quick work of the task, filling line after line with letter-like marks and then asking me to read what he had written (as would be the title of

Marie Clay's 1975 book, *What Did I Write?*). Others drew, some copied whatever words they could find in no particular order, and then there were those who sought out words to write a bit of a message. It was if I had stepped into another world – what was happening here?

In time, as I learned to set up daily writing and sharing routines and to respond to a diversity of child approaches to writing, I started to notice all the talk accompanying writing and, then, how wrapped up in children's worlds writing could become. To understand these latter phenomena, I would need to sit and watch, but not from the teacher perspective but from – best I could – the child perspective.

I wasn't sure how to do this but, at the University of Texas at Austin, I took an anthropology and education class with Doug Foley and learned about an ethnographic stance and a critical frame as well – working toward a more just world; then I took an applied sociolinguistic class with Celia Genishi (my good friend was in her first years of a professorship then, to my great luck), and I learned how language could reveal children's worlds, including children whose voices were ignored in the literature (e.g., children who spoke a disrespected vernacular). And I was on my way.

I have never stopped being curious about writing, which I think of now as a mediator of children's relationships, and the relationships that matter in school most definitely include those among peers.

Bobbie: Who were the early influences in your academic career that pushed your thinking about children's writing?

Anne: I would say the first academic influences (aside from the two people mentioned above) were not about children's writing but about language as a social tool – Dell Hymes especially and what was then the new field of sociolinguistics (and, of course, his colleague at the time, John Gumperz).

Then there were the folks following little children around with tape recorders, respecting their language – Roger Brown, Susan Ervin Tripp, and Courtney Cazden, a one time early childhood teacher too who has contributed so very much to our respect for classroom language. And certainly I read lots about (and knew from listening) the deficit language ideology applied to "other" children – Labov and Smitherman are two who influenced me in the seventies. Finally I have to mention Bill Corsaro, whom I met when I first went to Berkeley and who helped illuminate children's cultures.

As for writing, I was mesmerized by Marie Clay's books in the mid-seventies. She paid such careful attention to young children's production of text. I am of a different generation, so I am interested in how those text production decisions mediate children's social lives, but I learned to appreciate children's exploring of written text from Marie Clay. I knew from teaching that drawing was also important and there were scholars who located writing in children's use of other symbolic modes (an old but favorite is by Helen Eng).

And here I must mention Lev Vygotsky – *Mind in Society* was barely out but I read it when I was doing my dissertation and from Vygotsky I learned that, to understand writing, one had to see it within children's symbolic repertoire for representing and reconstructing and communicating about their worlds.

On a more practical side, I was inspired by Connie and Harold Rosen's book *The Language of Primary School Children*, whose chapter on children's writing I read and reread and read again. It was so practical and so child respectful –all about listening to a child and helping the child find a way into text and also about respecting children's playful interpretations of new kinds of writing tasks across the disciplines.

Perhaps because of my own humble roots – and my becoming a teacher in the late sixties early seventies, a time of great idealism among many of my generation – I have always been interested in children's resources that are not respected by the dominant ideology of school literacy (back to Labov, Smitherman, and Cazden too).

When I was organizing my dissertation, I kept reading about children speaking vernacular Englishes (especially African American kids) and emerging bilingualism. At this time, Graves was starting his studies of children's writing processes. I loved the respectful observation but still, I was finding my way out of the notion of a child author as an individual interacting with a paper into one of a child player, peer, and learner learning writing as a means of engaging with, and playing in, the world. So I was looking in another way. Sometimes realizing that one's path is different from another's is very useful – it pushes one to articulate and clarify one's path.

Later on, well into the eighties, I discovered Bakhtin on a table in a Berkeley bookstore and I felt my ways of looking at children expand. Voices answering voices, words echoing past conversations, people talking from somewhere addressing someone on their horizon – all of this helped me talk more confidently not only about writing as interaction but also about societal discourse of race, class, and gender – children were positioned in a world of differences but they were not stagnant representatives of some social group. We all move in space, finding different aspects of ourselves as we reach out to diverse others. The complexity of children of and in the experienced world became more manageable.

Bobbie: One of my favorite aspects of your writing is how you bring children to life. When I read your writing, I feel like I am in the classroom sitting next to you watching the scene unfold. I can feel the very unique and individual personalities of the different children. Do you have any particularly memorable experiences of the children?

Anne: Oh, I have lots of kids I remember like I knew them yesterday. I can measure out my adult life by the children I knew at one time and then the next. I get so close from that sitting and observing; I don't choose as focal children those who overly attend to me as opposed to their peers.

But still, I am not invisible. I am there "doing my job," as 6-year-old Jameel once said, and my job was "not to tell [him] what to do," as he explained to a peer he was annoying. Indeed, among the most memorable children was Jameel. He was a homeless child in the East Bay, initially kind of on edge, sensitive to being bumped or otherwise disregarded. But once he relaxed, this amazing child emerged; he used every bit of textual resource he had to imaginatively make a world on paper – cartoons from the TV, and commercials too (he had the used car salesman language down pat), soul songs, school books, and he could sometimes talk with the performative intensity of a preacher. When he was performative on paper, of course he didn't like his audience talking back. He called into question some taken-for-granted pedagogical practices – like the daily sharing time being conceived of as an editorial feedback time. Not for a performer.

I was fascinated by Jameel's playfulness with language, and he took to my interest in him. One day he was super excited because he was going to a pizza party for children who had had an especially great week in school. He told me this and then stopped, looked at me ever so sympathetically and said with great kindness "I don't think you're invited." (He is in *Social Worlds of Children Learning to Write*....)

Jameel did SO well in his first grade with his fabulous teacher but then he was taken from his mother and put in foster care; given this regulation and that one, it was impossible to find out where he was.

Years later, I asked a former student who was working for the district central office to try to find Jameel in the system. He found out that Jameel was attending an alternative high school for children who were having troubles in school. Such a smart child should not have been having troubles in school, but there it was.

I have had that experience more than once, of having young children with fabulous starts to schooling somehow defeated, not so much by academics, but by the experience of schooling amid life and its troubles. I dislike the rhetoric that if children somehow learn their letters and sounds at younger and younger ages, oh they'll progress through school with no troubles at all. Ridiculous.

Bobbie: The life that you bring to the children on paper often begins with your titles. You often quote them or use their words in the titles. Just to name a few titles:

"N spell my grandmama"

"Oh ppbbt!"

"I'm gonna express myself"

Donkey Kong in Little Bear Country

The stolen lipstick of overheard song

The case of the singing scientist

How do you come up with fantastic titles that capture the heart and soul of the piece that you are writing?

Anne: Oh thanks so much for the compliment. I don't have any particular strategies. A child will say something that keeps reverberating in my head as I think about the project (Jameel referring to himself as a "singing scientist") or an image will appear that can be translated into words (Noah's drawing of *Donkey Kong in Little Bear Country*). Book publishers seem to like straight forward titles for educational books. Not so much space for play.

Bobbie: I was a classroom teacher in the late 1990s and now I am a teacher educator. It's interesting to see how so many things have remained the same when it comes to writing in school, especially in the lower elementary grades. My two children brought home workbooks pages that I could have given to my students when I was a classroom teacher.

And my undergraduate and graduate students want to give their students similar types of workbooks pages. In working with pre-service and in-service teachers, I find that they want to teach in a way that is 'safe' for them or teach 'what they know or what they experienced' instead of trying to push the boundaries of their own comfort level.

What advice do you have for teachers and teacher educators that can help them move away from traditional workbook-style teaching to seeing writing as part of a permeable curriculum?

Anne: Well, there are three ideas that are important for me and perhaps may be helpful to others:

First, writing is an intention-driven symbolic tool, through which we participate in particular kinds of social events.

What drives writing – what makes working to orchestrate this complex system worth it – is an intention. So this means, skills are just skills, writing is communication. So, from the beginning this matters. The little ones often chat with each other as they write, sometimes developing complex kinds of play within which the writing and drawing play a role. (There are lots of examples of this in *ReWRITING the Basics*; my favorite example is two little kindergarteners who are "playing sisters, on paper" – one adds the other to her drawn family and then writes [with mock writing combined with the other child's exactly written name] about how she loves her "best sister.")

If we do not let the children talk when they write, we may get no writing; the intentional context may be destroyed, along with the help and feedback children offer each other. If we have a daily sharing time, children may anticipate that sharing time and whether or not others will laugh or otherwise like their work.

Second, as Jimmy Britton said, we as teachers can't teach children we don't know. This makes teacher observation basic to teaching writing.

We can learn of children's interests and their chosen companions or what language they use to comfortably discuss their writing or even collaborate during writing in some way. We learn about the social arrangements that prevail when they are most participatory – small groups? of which children?; pairs? of which children? We may learn too about their chosen symbolic tools for representing. (how might writing be incorporated in multimodal productions – comics? digital stories? murals or collages? picture books?)

Obvious in what has been said, I do not think we should look at children only in terms of some checklist of competencies. We have to know our children as human beings with interests, dispositions, friends and avoided peers, symbolic preferences (drawing, singing, dancing, sculpting), and particular sensitivities, based, perhaps, on their sociopolitical position in society or particular complexities of home life. If we know our children, then we can figure out possible social arrangements (kids can collaborate, for example), possible genres, including multimodal ones, particular inquiry projects that children may find compelling for the daily writing period or for writing across the curriculum.

Finally, teaching means, within one's goals,

responding to and building on what children are trying to do.

Whatever our plans, if the bulk of children's writing time does not include intentional writing – intentional being defined from children's view point – supported by their teacher and their collegial peers, then, in the end, we are not teaching writing at all.

Bobbie: You began your teaching career in 1972 and then received your Ph.D. in 1981. How has the research on children's writing evolved since that time?

Anne: I do want to begin by saying that I think researchers interested in children's writing – and contributing to our collective knowledge – should, in my view, do two things:

(a) know the literature in the area and, also, the particular theoretical and conceptual tools that particular research literature has used; and

(b) locate the studied children in the complexities of how the children are situated in society.

The latter has definitely evolved dramatically in the research area on children's writing. I remember when I ventured into doctoral work, there were articles being published with titles like "the six-year-old writer" and some such. Not only is there no one path into writing, and no one "six-year-old writer," our children, like children the world over, are specific individuals located in particular sociocultural and geographic locales and carrying particular cultural resources (chief among them, their languages but also their experiences with varied sorts of texts, whatever their medium); too, their teachers are under varied pressures to teach and demand particular kinds of academic performances.

When we read research, we want to know, how are these children located in the sociocultural and linguistic world? And since their knowledge of school writing will be formed through particular educational activities, what is the teacher's curriculum like and what pressures is she under (e.g., to have children pick out from a selection the correctly punctuated sentence – since that will be on a test). I think our expectations as readers of research are more sophisticated now. We need all this information, since any generalizations to be made will depend on comparison of children engaging in writing activities across settings.

Another change, I think, has been a widening interest in children's engagement with and use of popular culture. I can go back to the early studies I did in grad school in the late seventies – they are full of popular culture, but it never occurred to me to ask questions about what children's participation in popular culture meant to the children themselves, as well as to their teachers. This was most certainly to change (e.g., *Writing Superheroes*).

There is now a recognition that contemporary childhoods tend to be infused with the popular media (although that media will vary across geographic and sociocultural sites; for example, in my current global project on children learning to write, children in a Kenyan village did not have access to television, but they did listen to the radio; that radio was the source of their popular songs; few U.S. studies would highlight the radio as a central media source for child affiliation and pleasure [although it certainly was among the children in *The Brothers and Sisters Learn to Write*].)

Related to this has been the interest in issues of young children's use of digital media –the media itself or the experience of engagement with the media – in their ventures into writing. These studies in the U.S. have not usually been located in low income communities, where I think access to particular media may be limited by economics. Still, I think studies that plan projects to engage children with composing tools via computer and tablets are interesting – they may demonstrate new possibilities, particularly for multimodal composing.

Finally, I want to comment on the changing role of drawing and, more broadly, multimodality. When I first began my studies, drawing was seen as a temporary form of "writing," to be replaced by written text. This no longer makes sense. I think (tied to the comments above) now there is an interest in how children differentiate their symbolic repertoire, so that they understand the particular strengths and limits of varied symbolic tools.

Bobbie: What do you think about the state of education today?

Anne: I think it should be a time of excitement – when child agency is realized across the curriculum through inquiry projects, even as the arts play a huge role as playful children are guided into new forms of expression and learning. But it is not. I think, spurred on initially by No Child Left Behind, the push toward accountability through standardized tests narrowed the educational curriculum and contributed to the intensity of the push-down in isolated academic content.

Children are greeted into kindergarten with tests of letter names and sounds and, from the get go, may be judged as "bright" or "not" on the results of narrow testing before anybody's tried to get to know the children as human beings, players, friends, and learners, indeed, before anyone's tried to teach whatever it is judged as critical for young children to know and to learn. And play, that mainstay of child learning, may be absent from the kindergarten.

Narrow curricula that provide little space for children to negotiate their ways into school activities and that provide a crimped view of who children are and what they know may eliminate children from powerful learning from the get go. I know there are teachers and programs that are full of lively, engaged children. But too often, there is a mandated "pedagogy of poverty" (to borrow Martin Haberman's phrase), of low level teaching of aspects of literacy that allow no agency for children to figure out what literacy is about and how it works and how it can work for them as children.

I just returned from a trip to South Africa; in the township schools, children were being taught through a rote recitation method the conventions of English literacy; in the more affluent city school that I visited, there was lively engagement of children in all manner of activity – and there was play. Some children are being taught superficial facts and to follow orders; others are being socialized as agents of inquiry and public expression. This has been true in may own lifetime when I read as a teacher-to-be the appalling book by Bereiter and Engelmann *Teaching Disadvantaged Children in the Preschool*, with its breathtaking ignorance of language, literacy, and sociocultural difference.

We all still have work to do.

I take inspiration from the educational reformer Deborah Meier, who, in her book *The Power of Their Ideas*, talked about how the kindergarten – the old fashioned kindergarten – was a model for all of education. Attention to imaginative play and to making friends is the beginning of empathetic concern for the world and the capacity to imagine it differently.

"As we eliminate from our schools and from children's after-school lives the time and space for exercising their creative imagination and building personal ties, we've cheated our children and our society in a far more critical way than we're inclined to understand" (Meier, 1995, p. 63).

Bobbie: For those who are interested in researching and studying children's writing, what advice would you give them?

Anne: There is room for all kinds of work on children's writing. I think, though, that what is key is understanding that the heart of the story is not on the page but in the world being mediated by the page. Observational skills matter. And the observer cannot attend only to one child writing but to the larger social happening in which the child is (or is not) participating by means of that writing.

If writing is situationally merely a task or a set of rote skills, then the researcher may have no access to children's intentions, agency, and social lives, nor, in fact, to composing at all. Of course, in the cracks of the curriculum, children may be found composing as part of their unofficial worlds – love letters (and their opposite), birthday party invites, funny stories …

Bobbie: What areas of further research would you like to see in the area of children's writing?

Anne: I think all the trends mentioned above are good ones. As for me, I have just finished a project (I believe I already mentioned it) in which children's early entry into school and school writing was described as it unfolded in 8 very different sites around the globe.

I think the notions of how children move into writing are too narrow, given that ideologies of childhoods, schooling, and writing itself are different across the globe, as are children's textual resources. Finding common themes and different articulations of child writing is to the benefit of us all; narrow notions of how children begin, of useful resources, of "best" home supports leave some children's entry into composing outside the realm of curricular imagination.

Most of all, I would like to see researchers approach children's writing as embedded in their lives as friends, players, and scholars across the curriculum. The questions then open up, limited only by the researchers' curiosity and imagination.

A Bibliography of Anne Haas Dyson's Most Recent Publications

Books

Dyson, A. H. (Ed.) (2016). *Child cultures, schooling, and literacy: Global perspectives on composing unique lives*. New York, NY: Routledge.

Dyson, A.H. (2013). *ReWRITING the basics: Literacy learning in children's cultures*. New York, NY: Teachers College Press.

Genishi, C., & Dyson, A. H. (2009). *Children, language, and literacy: Diverse learners in diverse times*. New York, NY and Washington, DC: Teachers College Press & The National Association for the Education of Young Children.

Dyson, A. H., & Genishi, C. (2005). *On the case: Approaches to language and literacy research*. New York, NY: Teachers College Press.

Dyson, A. H. (2003). *The brothers and sisters learn to write: Popular literacies in childhood and school cultures.* New York, NY: Teachers College Press.

Journal Articles and Book Chapters

Dyson, A. H. (2015). The search for inclusion: Deficit discourse and the erasure of childhoods. *Language Arts*, 92, 199-207.

Genishi, C., & Dyson, A. H. (2014). Play as the precursor of literacy development. In E. Brooker, M. Blais & S. Edwards (Eds.), *Sage handbook of play and learning* (pp. 228-239). London, UK: SAGE.

Dyson, A. H. (2013). The case of the missing childhoods: Methodological notes for composing children in writing studies. *Written Communication*, 30, 399-427.

Dyson, A. H., & Dewayani, S. (2013). Writing in childhood cultures. In K. Hall, T. Cremin, B. Comber, & L. Moll (Eds.), *International handbook of research on children's literacy, learning, and culture* (pp.258-274). Oxford, UK: Wiley-Blackwell.

Dyson, A. H. & Genishi, C. (2013). Social talk and imaginative play: Curricular basics for young children's language & literacy. In N. Unrau & D. Alvermann (Eds.), *Theoretical models and processes of reading, 6th edition* (pp. 164-181).

Newark, DE: International Reading Association.

Dyson, A. H. (2013). Staying in the (curricular) lines: Practice constraints and possibilities in childhood writing. In M. Prinsloo & M. Baynham (Eds.), *Literacy studies, Volume IV: Literacy in education and at work* (pp. 107-144). Thousand Oaks, CA: Sage.

Dyson, A. H. (2012). Relations between oral language and literacy. In C. Chapelle (Ed.), *The encyclopedia of applied linguistics*. Indianapolis, IN: Wiley-Blackwell.

Dyson, A. H. (2012). Ethical worlds of school children's writing cultures: Individualism meets dialogism. In S. Matre, D.K. Sjohelle & R. Solheim (Eds.), *To find one's own voices, to express oneself and receive answers: Theoretical and analytical perspectives on textual work in the classroom* [English translation from Norwegian] (pp.93-100). Oslo: Universitetsforlaget Publishing House.

Dyson, A. H. (2012). The place of childhoods in school writing programs: A matter of ethics. In J. Larson & J. Marsh (Eds.), *The Sage handbook of early childhood literacy*, 2nd edition (pp. 485-500). London, UK: Sage.

Genishi, C., & Dyson, A. H. (2012). Racing to the top: Who's accounting for the children? In B. Ayers, J. Siln & G. Boldt (Eds.), *Challenging the politics of the teacher accountability movement: Toward a more hopeful educational future.* Occasional Paper 27 [Online]. New York, NY: Bank Street College. (http://bankstreet.edu/occasionalpapers)

Genishi, C., Dyson, A. H., & Russo, L. (2011). Playful learning: Early education that makes sense to children. In B. S. Fennimore & A. Lin Goodwin (Eds.), *Promoting social justice for young children* (pp. 59-70). New York, NY: Springer.

Dyson, A. H., & Genishi, C. (2011). The buzz on teaching and community. In V. Kinloch (Ed.), *Urban literacies: Critical perspectives on language, learning, and community* (pp. 91-94). New York, NY, Teachers College Press.

Dyson, A. H. (2010). The cultural and symbolic "begats" of child composing: Textual play and community membership. In O. Saracho & B. Spodek (Eds.), *Language and cultural diversity in early childhood education* (pp.191-211). Charlotte, NC: Information Age Publishing.

Dyson, A. H. (2010). Writing childhoods under construction: Revisioning "copying" in early childhood. *Journal of Early Childhood Literacy, 10,* 7-31.

Dyson, A. H. (2010). Opening curricular closets in regulated times: Finding pedagogical keys. *English Education, 42,* 307-319.

Dyson, A. H. (2010). Childhoods left behind? Official

and unofficial basics of child writing. In N. Yelland (Ed.), *Critical issues in early childhood*, Vol. 2. (pp. 159-176). London. UK: Routledge.

Anne Haas Dyson

A Short Biography

Anne Haas Dyson, Ph.D., began her career in education as an elementary school teacher at the El Paso Catholic Diocese in El Paso, Texas in 1972. In 1974, she moved to the Austin Independent School District in Austin, Texas, where she taught as a substitute teacher and, later, as a preschool teacher in a Title 1 Migrant Program and, finally, as a first grade and ESL teacher in bilingual programs.

Dyson received her Ph.D. in Education from the University of Texas in Austin, Texas in 1981. It was during her time at University of Texas, Austin that she connected her classroom teaching experiences with her doctoral work and became interested in the social and cultural worlds of childhood writers.

In 1984, she published her first book with her good friend and colleague Celia Genishi titled Language Assessment in the Early Years. Since this first publication, Dyson has published 12 books. Her most recent book is an edited volume titled Child Cultures, Schooling, and Literacy: Global Perspectives on Composing Unique Lives, which was published by Routledge, Taylor and Francis Group in 2016. Dyson's latest book features her collaborative global research project on children learning to write. In addition, Dyson has written over 100 journal articles and book chapters all regarding children's writing.

Dyson is Faculty Excellence Professor in the College of Education at the University of Illinois at Urbana/Champaign. Prior, Dyson has held positions at Michigan State University (2002-2006), the University of California, Berkeley (1984-2002), and the University of Georgia (1981-1985).

Dyson has been awarded numerous grants from the Spencer Foundation to study the social and cultural worlds of childhood writers. She has also received a number of awards for her scholarship and contributions to the field of education. Awards for her writing include the John Hayes Award for Excellence in Writing Research (2014, 2009), Janet Emig Award from the National Council of Teachers of English (NCTE; 2006, 2002) and the Purves Award from NCTE (1999). Dyson received the Early Literacy Educator of the Year Award from NCTE (shared with co-author Celia Genishi, 2012), the Distinguished Teaching Award of the University of California-Berkeley (1998) and the Promising Researcher Award for NCTE (1982).

In 2015, Dyson received a second NCTE David H. Russell Award for Distinguished Research (the first received in 1993). In addition, with Celia Genishi, she received the prestigious Outstanding Educator of the Year Award from NCTE. This award recognizes the distinguished careers of Dyson and Genishi and their major contributions to the field of English Language Arts.

Bobbie Kabuto

A Short Biography

Bobbie Kabuto, PH.D., is Associate Professor of Literacy Education in the Elementary and Early Childhood Education Department at Queens College, City University of New York. She teaches and advises in the B-6 Literacy Program that leads to New York State certification as a B-6 Reading Teacher.

Her research interests include the relationships among early bi/literacy, socially constructed identities, and language ideologies. She currently works with families of struggling beginning readers and writers.

Her work has been highlighted in journals such as *The Reading Teacher*, *The Journal of Early Childhood Literacy*, and *Early Childhood Research and Practice*. Her book *Becoming Biliterate: Identity, Ideology, and Learning to Read and Write in Two Languages* was published by Taylor and Francis in July 2010.

58390763R00065

Made in the USA
Lexington, KY
09 December 2016